CLASSIC & MODERN
SIGNATURE STYLES

ALAN BARLIS • DENNIS WEDLICK

INTRODUCTION BY JULIE V. IOVINE

Published by
ORO Editions
Publishers of Architecture, Art, and Design
Gordon Goff: Publisher
www.oroeditions.com
info@oroeditions.com

Copyright © 2013 by ORO Editions
ISBN: 978-1-935935-88-9
10 09 08 07 06 5 4 3 2 1 First edition

Photography:
Reto Guntli & Agi Simoes: 2, 3, 37-49, 51-59, 61-71, 73-81, 119, 125-137,
149-157, 159-167, 183-197, 199-213, 216
Peter Aaron/Esto: Front Cover, Back Cover, 1, 8, 17, 23-35, 83-91,
93-113, 139-147
Ezra Stoller/Esto: 15
Van Jones Martin: 117
Aaron Zebrook: Portrait
Courtesy Architectural Digest, photographed by Peter Aaron/Esto: 169-181

Illustrations:
George Shear: 12, 114
Jessica Young Goldvarg: 20-21, 122-123

Architecture: Barlis Wedlick Architects

Interior Design:
Barlis Wedlick Architects and as noted:
Thad Hayes, Inc.: 93-113
J. Doyle Design Inc.: 169-181
White Webb, LLC: 139-147, 199-213
Pierce Allen: 183-197

Editor: Mary Murfitt
Graphic Design: Wayne-William Creative, Inc
Production Assistant: Manjola Gjini

This book was printed and bound using a variety of sustainable
manufacturing processes and materials including soy-based inks, acqueous-
based varnish, VOC- and formaldehyde-free glues, and phthalate-free
laminations. The text is printed using offset sheetfed lithographic printing
process in (book specific) color on 157gsm premium matte art paper with an
off-line gloss acqueous spot varnish applied to all photographs.

ORO Editions makes a continuous effort to minimize the overall carbon
footprint of its publications. As part of this goal, ORO Editions, in
association with Global ReLeaf, arranges to plant trees to replace those used
in the manufacturing of the paper produced for its books. Global ReLeaf
is an international campaign run by American Forests, one of the world's
oldest nonprofit conservation organizations. Global ReLeaf is American
Forests' education and action program that helps individuals, organizations,
agencies, and corporations improve the local and global environment by
planting and caring for trees.

Library of Congress data: pending

For information on our distribution, please visit our website
www.oroeditions.com

CLASSIC & MODERN

Classic & Modern: Signature Styles presents a portfolio of homes with one-of-a-kind styles derived from the personalities, tastes and narratives of those that live within. Each home is accompanied by a story that explains how the homeowners arrived at their own signature style and how that style translated into the creation of their personal "dream home." The goal of the book is to inspire others to discover their own signature style. The examples in this book reveal not only the expressive art of architecture but also the importance of creating a "good home"—one that is based on the principles of good design, has character, blends comfort with practicality and is sensitive to its environment.

As an architect, when I meet a new client, I wonder what their signature style might be: Are they minimalists at heart or the more romantic type? Would they be most comfortable in clean, crisp, modern spaces filled with natural light or classic rooms filled with texture and history? More often than not, people's personal style is often a bit of both. Most people are attracted to various qualities of different architectural styles and cannot easily be defined as minimalist or romantic, modern or classic. This is why our firm believes that every client we meet has his or her own *signature style*. Phrases like "New Old House," "Retro Modern" and "East West Style" are popular journalistic descriptions of the turn-of-the-twenty-first-century residential designs that fuse ideas from the traditions of modern and classic architecture. The homes we are presenting here do exactly that.

The homes are divided into two portfolios: designs that are mostly Modern in their overall character and those that are primarily Classic. All are unique and represent how, once a person identifies a style that appeals to them, he or she can personalize it to create their signature style. Even though these designs emulate either modern or classic styles, they deviate from the expected to the creative by incorporating not only the narrative and aspirations of the homeowners but the physical location of the home itself.

The first portfolio, Signature Modern Styles, is represented by five households. The second portfolio presents eight homes built from Signature Classic Styles. All the homes are both classic and modern concurrently, and each one tells a story that we hope will inspire and empower you to create a meaningful and innovative signature style home of your own.

TABLE OF CONTENTS

PART II: SIGNATURE CLASSIC PAGE 114

IN THE NOW

JULIE V. IOVINE

For today's homeowner, the exhilarating opportunity to build a new home has a daunting side that was not a factor in the past. For starters, practically every imaginable approach is open to explore. And that can be as scary as a blank page. New homebuilders face the most basic questions from scratch: Does my home define who I am or who I wish to be? What story does it tell, for now and in the future?

In the past, the answer was fairly simple: one had to build appropriately according to one's station...geographically, socially, economically and in some corners, also according to political and religious affiliations. How to proceed was completely and clearly established before the first blueprint was inked and the last plank laid.

That was the strait jacket from which modernism was determined to break. In the process, however, new restrictions arose, in their own way every bit as limiting as the old rules. The modern movement, by insinuating that drawing ideas, shapes and styles from the past was somehow illegitimate and had to be supplanted by a vigorous embrace of new technology, implicitly denied the importance of family life and its resonances rooted in personal rites, memories and rituals threading back through the years.

Drawing a line between past and a future-facing present was not only arbitrary but a damaging kind of self-effacement. Following a brief period of acquiescence, many simply ignored the stricter tenets of modernism, hastening its transformation from a mandate to a style. We continue to wrestle with how best to give shape to our lives, especially when designing those most intimate of places, our homes. Even Philip Johnson whose Glass House in New Canaan, Connecticut, is the aesthetic ideal of the modern house, kept his art collection, his house guests and even his life partner, David Whitney, in more traditionally inspired spaces elsewhere on the property.

With history fully accessible, up to and including modernity, the important question becomes: What does it mean to be "contemporary"?

As Alan Barlis and Dennis Wedlick present with such clarity in *Classic & Modern: Signature Styles,* the underpinning fundamentals of good design have always been constant: Proportion, Scale and Light. Understanding how to establish the most pleasing relationships for these essential qualities creates the framework that allows all other choices to fall more easily into place.

Confidence in manipulating, even playing with these principles, is a mark of a contemporary approach. The window placements, for instance, at the Stanfordville Residence have neither the symmetry required of a classical design nor the strip-formation of a modern vocabulary. Instead, they are asymmetrical and opportunistic in order to capture the best views of the rolling Upstate landscape.

To be truly contemporary has often meant pushing the latest technological methods. Here, too, Wedlick and Barlis broaden that definition, combining the prefabricated and the handcrafted in the same project, as they did for a house in Claverack where trusses were prefabricated and the stone hand-stacked. The repositioning of technology to include both the factory-generated and individually crafted is a decisively appropriate way to think about incorporating technologies for a richer future.

Sustainability is, of course, a major contemporary concern in building long-term efficiency into homes. Vernacular homes in rural settings were always very sensitive to matters of natural insulation, solar heat gain by orientation with compass points, air circulation and built-in shading devices. Today's architect can choose between high-tech systems for monitoring and adjusting energy use and the more passive constructs as favored in many of the houses in *Signature Styles.* The key here is to follow the most nimbly flexible approach. As ever, "both/and" is better than "either/or."

Personal narrative has emerged as an area of especial interest in defining what is contemporary. In our mobile society where heirlooms are less likely to be passed down and even homesteads rarely go more than three generations deep, storytelling is an important way to anchor meaning to place.

It is perhaps where *Signature Styles* most excels, enabling clients to filter their resonant memories through the principles of design with a goal to creating high-functioning contemporary homes loaded with layers of meaning. Each story told in *Signature Styles* reverberates with the engagement of client and architect striving to achieve the most effective balance.

But my personal favorite is the story about two salt box-inspired wings jointed at an angle by a glassed-in living space with a deep modern overhang. That simple device allows for shaded refuge in the summer and a space drenched in low-angled light in winter, acting as a portal for warm air to infiltrate both wings. The freedom to combine old and new and to find the angle that works for the individual without compromising the whole is perhaps, above all, the hallmark of the contemporary at its best.

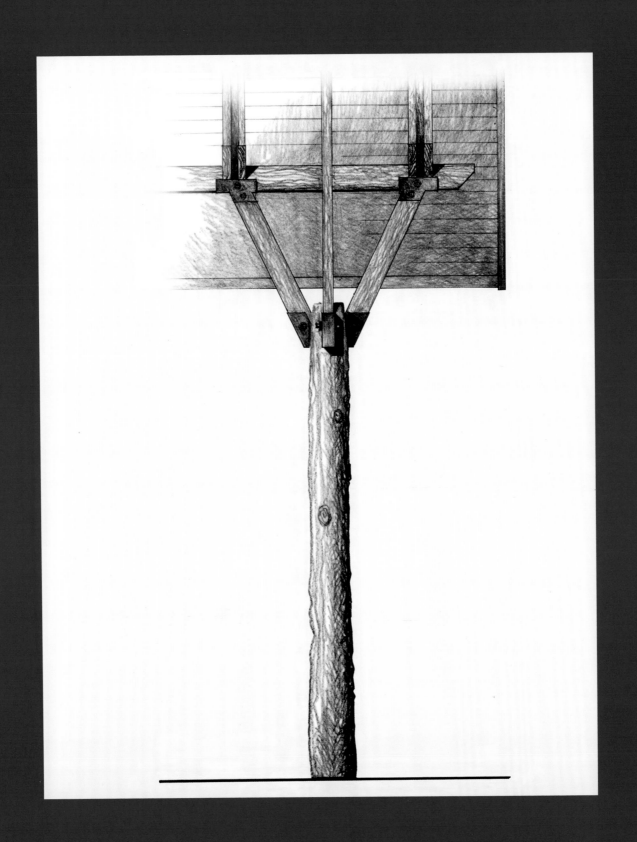

PART I
SIGNATURE MODERN

SIGNATURE MODERN STYLES
FUTURISTIC. UNSENTIMENTAL. MINIMALIST.

The quintessential example of the "Modern Style" is the Wiley Residence. Designed by Philip Johnson in 1956, it was certainly "futuristic" at the time. Understated, unsentimental yet elegant, the Wiley Residence appears as little more than a glass and steel box sitting atop a basic stone foundation. Its interiors are crisp, white-on-white, minimalist spaces animated only with an abundance of natural light and expansive views of nature.

Johnson is admired for elevating basic structural components, such as concrete, glass, sheets of metal and the fasteners that tie them together, into works of art with an enduring appeal. The Wiley Residence represents the best components of Modern Style: the comfort of bright, airy spaces; the delight of connectivity with nature; and the captivating beauty of the basic building blocks of architecture. It also exemplifies how the iconic modern home is stripped of any picturesque or romantic architectural elements such as wrap-around porches, oculus-shaped windows or steeply pitched roofs. The Signature Modern Style homes presented here are modern in many respects but more sentimental than the Wiley Residence. Woven into the design are regional, playful or even traditional architectural elements that Johnson would eschew.

Though it was inspired by the Wiley home, the Stanfordville Residence shown here beautifully illustrates how a modern signature style incorporates traditionally modern elements with the more familiar and classic.

This 1950s home is the Wiley Residence. It is perhaps the finest example of mid-century modern style. Designed by Philip Johnson, this home meticulously follows the tenets of minimalism and functionalism. It is minimal in its design because it uses no ornamental architectural elements; the beauty of the design is derived from the simple functionality of the space and the elegant structure. The top half contains the living, dining and cooking areas and is built of little more than steel columns and large sheets of glass. The bottom half contains the sleeping areas and is built to be a simple stone plinth for the glass box to perch on.

Open Floor Plans

In 2002, Kelly Hnatt and Brad Randall built a home for themselves and their two well-loved dogs in Stanfordville, New York. As with all of the portfolio homes presented here, their personal story and aspirations drove its creation but the design owes much to the thinking behind the Wiley Residence. From the exterior, it might seem that the two homes are not at all similar but a side-by-side comparison of the floor plans reveal the stylistic similarities.

The floor plan of a home is an architect's guide to determine the style of a home. Nearly every part of the house is represented in this one drawing—from the construction of the exterior walls to the placement of the kitchen sink. The style of a home is the result of how you arrange these parts.

The Wiley Residence floor plan is emblematic of a modern home. The main living area of the house consists of one big room surrounded on all four sides by glass. This is an open floor plan, meaning there are no interior partitions separating the various activities of the household. You can see in the Stanfordville Residence floor plan what this design owes to the Wiley Residence: one large room surrounded by windows on all four sides. There are no hallways, nooks or traditional closets—nothing to close in the space. The life of the modern home: all of the entertaining, dining, cooking and hobbies are enjoyed in this one light and expansive loft-like space.

Connectivity to Nature

Both residences are built on bucolic farmland just north of New York City. Since there are no walls, the views across the space are beautiful and unobstructed, and the light that filters in countless windows over the course of the day reaches every corner of these modern interiors. A side-by-side comparison of the Wiley and Stanfordville interiors illustrates just how similar the designs of these two homes really are.

The Stanfordville Residence was designed and built nearly fifty years after the Wiley House but owes much of its modern character to the mid-century modern designs of Philip Johnson. The loft-like living space, the expansive use of glass and the exposed structural components are the attributes that make this a modern home. The familiar barn shape, barn woodwork and barn-colored windows are what make it a personal signature style.

From the outside, the Stanfordville house does not appear to have nearly as much glass to take in the views of the countryside as the Wiley Residence, but this is a trick of the eye. The iconic mid-century modern house uses floor-to-ceiling glass from end to end to create the panoramic views. The Stanfordville house alternates between floor-to-ceiling glass and giant windows that nearly touch the floor and ceiling, allowing for an exterior wall surface to surround it. Inside, between the floor-to-ceiling glass and giant windows, there is enough wall space to allow for an alternate appearance other than the basic glass box the modernist prefers. But the twenty-first-century floor plan demonstrates the wall space is so minimal at eye level that the same 360-degree view the Wiley design offers is achieved. To further ensure the interior of the main living space takes in even more of the view of the surrounding landscape and sky, both designs push the ceiling height up to two floors. By combining an open floor plan with higher ceilings and higher windows, an unobstructed connection to the outdoors is made—like living outside year round within the comfort of a modern home.

Captivating Beauty of Simple Architecture

Stanfordville Residence's familiar barn-like shape is where it diverges from the more abstract shape of the mid-century modern Wiley Residence. It is obvious that the design of this signature modern home is inspired by the simple, yet elegant, construction of old-world barns. Surprisingly, the design of the glassy Wiley Residence was as well.

Twelve years before we designed this home for Brad and Kelly, I was working for Philip Johnson. I once asked him what the inspiration was behind the design of the Wiley Residence. "Why the nearby barns, of course!" was his answer. The futuristic and minimalist design of the Wiley Residence was indeed derived from old-world barn architecture—one lofty room filled with hay above and the lower, earth-bound level where the cows slept. The upper level of the Wiley Residence is smaller than the lower level with an abstract, almost ghostly form conveying the impression that perhaps an old barn had burned down and the new glass and steel pavilion was built atop the ruins.

Even though the pitched-roof, wood clad barns on the Wiley's property inspired the design of the Residence, Philip Johnson shunned the familiar barn shape and materials. Conversely, the Stanfordville Residence embraces the barn architecture inside and out by fusing traditional exterior materials with a structural system that is evocative of a timber-framed barn. The bent wood trusses of the nineteenth-century rural architecture from the area inspired this modern version.

Like the Wiley household, Brad and Kelly used a very limited palette of colors and simple, yet impressive, structural elements to achieve a modern, minimalist look. Wrapped in silvery, weathered wood shingles and grey metals, with an untreated grey concrete foundation, their design completes the image of barn architecture while also maintaining the minimalist palette of a modernist. To suit their signature style, Brad and Kelly opted to paint the steel framing around the glass doors and floor-to-ceiling windows a bright barn-red for a pop of color and playfulness.

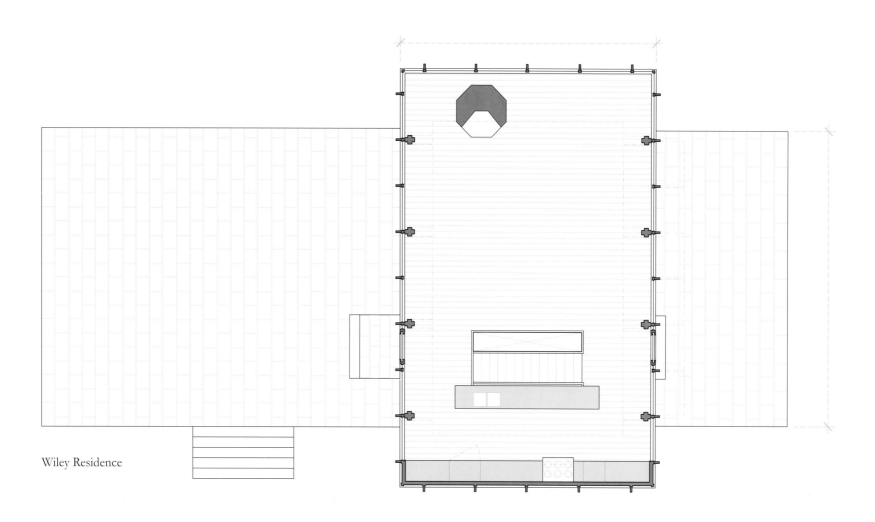

Wiley Residence

As you can see in this diagram, the floor plan is a road map to understanding the style of a home because so many architectural elements are spelled out and laid out here—from the construction of the walls to the placement of the kitchen sink. A comparison of the floor plan of the mid-century modern Wiley Residence and the twenty-first century modern Stanfordville Residence reveals that the two homes are built from obviously related layouts, only the latter has a larger living and dining area.

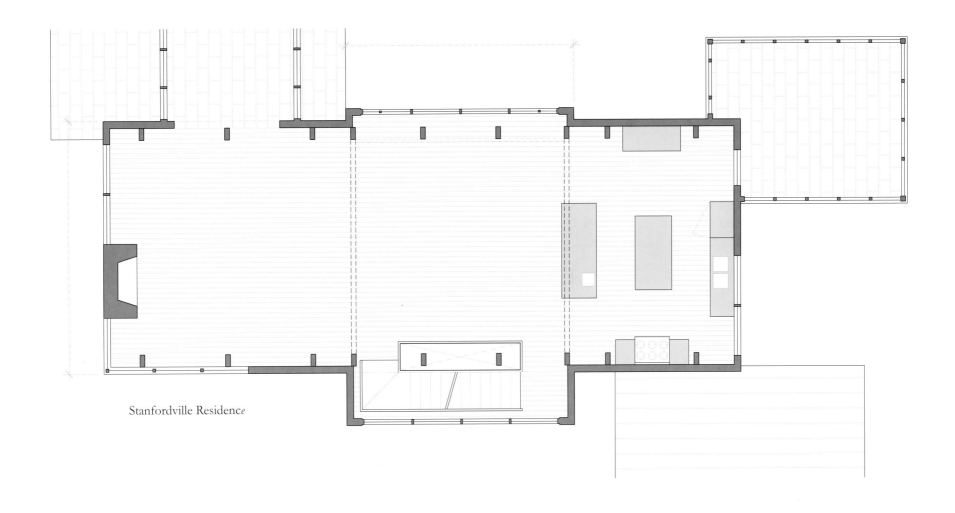

Stanfordville Residence

RURAL

A MODERNIST POLE BARN

pole barn is a minimal structure. It consists of a series of timbers driven into the ground then stitched together with beams to hold up the walls and roof. Siding and sheet metal are added to keep the elements out, and voilà—a pole barn. Many modernists love the simplicity of rural structures like these.

Kelly and Brad's affinity for modern art and minimalist architecture led us to create their signature style—a country dream home based on a modernist pole barn. There is very little to the structure that doesn't meet the eye. The wood beams in this modern pole barn design are formed into the shape of a wishbone and connected together with steel. Not much more is added other than siding, metal, insulation and wallboard. Sustainable materials, such as Douglas-fir prefabricated structural framing, Eastern White Cedar siding and bamboo flooring, were used throughout the house.

To complete our couple's signature style, the finishes inside and out are as unassuming and sparse as the structure itself. The exterior is primarily one color—grey; the interior—white. The only colors added to this minimalist palette are accents of red (the windows), orange (the wood floor and structure) and black (steel connections, granite counter top, etc.). The rooms are vaulted, resembling the interior of a picturesque barn, and the windows are asymmetrically arranged to take advantage of the beautiful views. The look of the fireplace, stairs and kitchen cabinetry is relaxed as opposed to the precision, factory-made aesthetic often found in a typical minimalist home.

The result of our collaboration: A modern-country dream home that reflects the signature style of the people who live there—smart and buttoned up without being minimalistically uptight.

RUSTIC

GREAT CAMP STYLE...BUT WITHOUT THE "CAMP"

*U*rbanites to the core, ironically, it was Alice and Richard's dream to build a rural refuge from the city. To them, this home would represent their retirement as an endless holiday for just the two of them and would, in the end, dissuade them from ever returning to the New York City social life.

Their signature style is built upon the Great Camp Style of the luxury Adirondack Mountain ranches and resorts. This version, however, eschews the bulkiness and heaviness of the nineteenth-century "log cabin" aesthetic typifying the original model. In other words, Alice and Richard wanted all the "Great" but none of the "Camp."

The exterior picks up the motifs of the Adirondacks using trademark autumnal colors, rural Americana details and, of course, logs. The colors here are softer and brighter shades than typically found in the Great Camp Style and the architectural features, though countrified, are not camp-like. The iconic "logs" at the entryway are minimalist chunks of trees stained a whimsical blue. In the spirit of the original Adirondack ranch resorts, which were constructed using sustainable native materials, we used locally sourced logs and stone. The design also included modern renewable materials and was carefully calibrated to take advantage of passive solar energy.

On the inside, the Great Camp Style influence is evident with soaring ceilings and walls of glass taking in views of nature. The owners' appreciation for the style can also be seen in the Arts and Crafts furnishings and memorabilia. However, you won't find the heavy wood paneling, blocky trim and log rafters typically used in classic Adirondack lodge interiors. These rooms feel light and open with white plaster walls, streamline trim and lightweight structural beams.

To fulfill this couple's desire that their home be spacious without being unnerving, we used architectural tricks such as arranging spaces along a cross axis, aligning doorways, eliminating hallways and using overlooks. Alice and Richard are never out of eyesight or earshot from each other and they never yearn to return to the city—a true testament to the transformational power of creating a signature style!

ORGANIC

DESIGN INSPIRED BY NATURE

century-old tree can be a beautiful work of organic architecture, especially when it consists of a complex trunk with broad branches that cantilever far from the trunk, displaying a remarkable structural design. A tree such as this is what drew Ron and Michael to this piece of land where they would build their weekend retreat from New York City.

Ron is a longtime admirer of the organic modern architecture of early modernists such as Charles and Henry Greene and Frank Lloyd Wright. All of these architects studied trees, rock ledges and other works of nature for inspiration for the structure and materials of their designs. Ron wanted to do the same for his woodland retreat. However, he didn't want a home that was too rustic, where the structure and materials actually looked like stone ledges and tree trunks. Ron's signature style employed concrete flooring, laminted wood trusses and milled wood walls to successfully capture and complement the colors, textures and sheen of nature's materials without mimicking them. The paint colors Ron uses—teal, orange and grey—further accomplish the same goal.

Unexpected accessories, like the steel and cable railings and industrial light fixtures, work well with this signature style even though they might seem more fitting in a SoHo loft as opposed to a Greene & Greene design. The most significant departure from Mr. Wright's designs is the home's open floor plan and cathedral ceilings. Though the early modernists were very fond of low-slung houses that blended into the landscape, there was a trade-off: low ceilings and short windows that minimized natural light and limited views of the outdoors. Conversely, the high ceilings in this design allow the maximum amount of daylight to penetrate through the tree tops and find its way indoors. And, thanks to the tall windows, the century-old tree that inspired Ron and Michael to create their retreat can be fully seen—from its base, to its crown and to each end of its widest branches.

MINIMALIST: TOWN & COUNTRY
COUNTRY MINIMALIST

There are two sides to performance artist Marina Abramovic. Her work demands restraint but her life as friend, mentor and activist is all about emotionality. This duality applies to her signature style as well. I call the two sides Spartan and Vivacious. We tapped into both in creating two homes for Marina—one in the city and one in the country.

Marina's simple words of direction: it must be spare (uncomplicated and functional, using nothing but white with no décor); it must be fun. The country home Marina asked us to help her renovate was a house we originally designed for another client ten years earlier. What appealed to Marina was the unexpected shape of the house. It was built in the shape of a star—a frequent icon used in her work.

We began by stripping away all the color and architectural elements within. Everything was whitewashed and all the decorative trim, window treatments and accessories were eliminated; even the natural pine flooring was stripped down to the raw wood. Interestingly, one doesn't perceive the star shape of Marina's house from the outside. It just looks like an unusually shaped house. Only on the inside, where the raw pine floors meet the newly painted bright white floors, is it apparent that each room is one point of a star. The second-floor rooms also have a pointed floor plate but the folded ceiling further reveals the star shape of the house.

Marina's colorful collection of vintage furniture and fun objects throughout her home really pop against the simple gallery-like white interior.

MINIMALIST: TOWN & COUNTRY
TOWN MINIMALIST

Marina's city house is a New York City loft in SoHo. It had been renovated in the 1980s but she did no remodeling after she bought it. Once again, Marina began with a vision of a clean, crisp space furnished with bursts of color. This was to be a one-room home—3,000 square feet large—where corners would be used for living, dining and sleeping. Somewhere in the middle, hidden in storage units, would be all other household needs. We suggested that this "somewhere-in-the-middle-zone" be created with colorful architecture. It would float in this all white apartment just like her colorful furniture floats in the all white rooms of her country home.

The result is a minimalist's loft with a splash of color at the core, which accommodates cooking, bathing and dressing areas. White frosted glass doors surround the core. When the doors are open the bright Crayola-colored contents are revealed but when the doors are closed, all is hidden away, returning the loft to a look of sparseness. Yet even with the opaque doors closed, the exotic colors and the activities within bleed through just enough to convey that, like Marina herself, vivaciousness and restraint can coexist beautifully in the same space.

ECO

STYLE MEETS CRAFTSMANSHIP & STEWARDSHIP

We include this design in our portfolio of Signature Modern homes because it showcases not only our firm's passion for Green architecture but also the skills of the owners, Bill and Meg, a builder and interior designer, respectively.

This home is part of the Claverack Homestead; a small community of environmentally sensitive homes master planned on historic farmland in the Hudson Valley. It is a Passive House...meaning it passively keeps the indoors comfortably warm or cool all year long without the aid of a heater or air-conditioner. This is the Greenest type of building. Tucked into the woods, this cottage, which at first may look like a conventional home, is both a state-of-the-art handmade and factory-built home. It is a case study in fusing traditional with modern architecture.

The house is made from hand-laid stone; crane-lifted prefabricated trusses and wall panels; hand-troweled concrete floors; and both shop-built and site-built millwork and cabinetry. The vast south-facing glass curtain wall connects the indoors to nature and works like a machine to passively heat the house with sunshine. All of these architectural features are structural highlights of a signature style of modernism that only master craftsmen, like Bill and his crew, could pull off.

Inside, the home is flooded with the warmth and the brightness of the sun thanks to the strategically placed windows that face south, west and east. The loft-like, open floor plan works in conjunction with a gently turning ceiling fan and heat-recovery ventilator, creating the feeling of fresh air flowing throughout the space at all times.

The traditional minimalist would be tempted to let the architecture steal the show by minimizing the furnishings, fixtures and colors. However, this signature home challenges that notion. The use of a complex blend of pastel colors, a myriad of natural wood finishes, from butternut cabinetry to yellow pine paneling, and an eclectic combination of accessories was the result of the collaboration of dozens of furnishing designers, local artisans and, of course, Meg, the homeowner herself.

RETRO

MANY SHADES OF MODERN

Fred and Nancy's Tribeca signature style penthouse is a blend of architectural styles: Art Deco, Art Moderne and Danish Modern. They culled through the design options presented to them by our firm and the interior designer to be sure that the end result would be an ideal balance of precision and craft—a trait they admire in art as well as architecture.

At first glance, the entry-stair hall seems to be lifted straight from the pages of a Manhattan Art Deco guidebook but a closer look reveals that the space is without the glitzy, trademark embellishments of Art Deco. A sweeping, curving staircase leads upstairs to a lacquered wall gallery that is more reminiscent of minimalist Art Moderne than the Art Deco movement it paralleled. Soft, deep shades of grey tie the two spaces together and set a tone of subdued elegance.

Danish Modern-inspired wood paneling and shelving are used as handcrafted accent walls in the library, den and guest master. Elsewhere, walls of mosaics, silk and wood were added to provide a stimulating break to the otherwise pristine modern décor.

The dazzling views of New York City and an important art collection take center stage in the design of this duplex penthouse thanks to two-story windows that wrap the entire penthouse and ceilings that seem to float in the air by being architecturally "pulled away" from the wall.

Interior designer Thad Hayes' and color consultant Donald Kaufman's interior décor melds with the architecture, successfully creating a quiet, yet comfortable and elegant, backdrop to the city and the art.

PART II
SIGNATURE CLASSIC

SIGNATURE CLASSIC
HISTORICAL. ORNAMENTAL. ROMANTIC.

Classic Styles are best known for being time-honored, ornamental and romantic. Each classic style uses a precise vocabulary of decorative architectural elements to generate an impression, continue traditions or create fantasies. Classic homes are created by building all the house parts according to that vocabulary. They must use the correct shapes, proportions and character for doors, windows, columns—even the layout of the rooms is prescribed by the classic style.

The classic Gothic Stick Style, for example, uses house parts that are reminiscent of fairytale architecture—the cottages and castles illustrated in children's storybooks— giving them a dreamy, idyllic character. The classic Adirondack Style is built from natural wood elements, seemingly hand-carved from solid tree trunks in order to give a rustic impression. Classic Greek Revival's vocabulary includes finely crafted architectural details based on rules of proportion dating back to ancient Greece. Tapping into these classic conventions in the design of a modern home convey the owner is knowledgeable and sophisticated enough to appreciate them.

It may seem, when compared to minimalist modern styles, the historic classic styles were much more elaborate and required more effort in bringing them about but in truth, recreating a classic style home is simply a matter of framing a roof, milling a wood porch post and laying out a plaster ceiling according to specific historic guidelines. The challenge is in the artistic execution of those details. The classic styles are greatly admired for their presence of character but they are, by their very nature, frozen in the time they were conceived.

The Signature Classic Style homes we are presenting here are modern interpretations of classic styles, designed to suit the predilections and lifestyle of a twenty-first-century household. To illustrate how these signature styles are both classic and modern, let's compare our best example of a Modern-Classic home (known by us as the River House) with the Millford Plantation—one of the historic Greek Revival homes we used for its inspiration.

Built in 1840 by Nathaniel F. Potter, the Millford Plantation in South Carolina is perhaps the finest example of a Greek Revival Style home in America. It adheres to every tenet of this neoclassical style. The Millford Plantation is listed on the National Register of Historic Places.

Perhaps the finest example of a Greek Revival Style home in America is the Millford Plantation in South Carolina. Built in 1840 by Nathaniel F. Potter, it strictly adheres to the tenets of this neoclassical style. The home is listed on the National Register of Historic Places and has been beautifully preserved over the years.

The exterior of the Millford Plantation house reveals how the Classical Revival guidelines work. The porch post height, diameter, decorative detailing and spacing are all ideal examples of the ornamental vocabulary required to create a Classical Revival house. By following these patterns, the nineteenth-century builder created what is recognizable as a Greek Revival home to anyone today who appreciates neoclassical architecture.

Many clients who admire historic homes like the Millford Plantation have come to us wondering if it is possible to build a modern home that taps into the decorative elements of the neoclassical vocabulary. In 2008, we set out to do exactly that when we designed the River House—a modern home guided by a Greek Revival vocabulary.

Our intention in designing this new home was never to replicate a historic Greek Revival but rather to carry on the traditions of neoclassical architecture while refitting them to suit modern family life.

Nearly all of the patterns used in the design and building of the River House come from the same traditional Greek Revival pattern books used to design Millford. However, the plans of a nineteenth-century plantation house would work for few modern families. In those days, servants prepared food in faraway kitchens. After dinner, all the men would retire to one parlor to smoke while the women gathered in a separate parlor to crochet. The best way to demonstrate the push and pull challenge of pursuing a Modern-Classic style is by comparing the plans of the River House and Millford. Though the size and shape of the individual rooms of both the modern and historic homes follow the same rules of proportion, the designs are as different as can be.

The plan of the Millford Plantation house is the result of a nineteenth-century lifestyle and the rules of neoclassical architecture. An even pair of parlors, each used by various members of the family according to old-world rules of society, flank a wide center-hall colonial. Symmetry plays a heavy role in the layout of the living spaces because it is one of the primary guidelines of the Revival Style. The Millford plan is identifiable as Greek Revival because there are an equal number of rooms on each half of the house. The kitchen is way off in a separate wing, creating an elegant symmetry in the center-hall portion of this majestic home.

The River House, inspired by the Millford Plantation, carries on the architectural traditions of the Greek Revival Style house. However, it was designed to be appropriate for a modern-day family. The porch posts, entablatures and overall proportions are straight from the Greek Revival Style patterns. The all-glass wall that slips behind the classical façade is purely a modern intervention. The interior is equally a blend of classic and modern, giving this home its own signature look.

The River House plan shows rooms sized according to the same proportions as Millford but the symmetry is forfeited in this layout. This is a modern design in which the rooms serve multiple functions rather than a single dedicated function. In the River House, book reading, dining, homework, bill paying and listening to music all happen in the same room, often at the same time. All of the functions of the River House, including the kitchen functions, are accommodated in just two asymmetrical rooms as compared to the five rooms (center hall, parlor, parlor, parlor, dining room) in the historic Millford where the kitchen is forced into a separate wing to preserve the required symmetry.

Creating the Classical Impression

From the first step inside, Greek Revival homes feel very formal. The front porch is designed to give the impression of a ceremonial building, like the Parthenon. That is why Greek Revival homes, banks and churches look so alike. All are based on the same patterns from the civic architecture of ancient Greece.

The design for the River House sets out to prove that it is possible to continue the traditions of classic architecture while shedding some of the formality. Though a formal center entry hall is a hallmark of historic Greek Revival homes, modern households tend to come and go from a door near the kitchen and rarely use a formal center hall. In our River House, the front door opens to a small foyer that leads straight into the kitchen where friends and family tend to congregate these days. Nonetheless, the River House achieves its formality by carrying on the traditions of classical proportions in every detail—where width, length and height are all dictated by the strict set of rules of neoclassical architecture. Since the days of ancient Greece, these rules of proportion are the measure for building beautiful rooms.

Once the size and the shape of our modern rooms were determined in accordance with the proper traditional proportions, the design of the River House was ready to be fitted out with the appropriate ornamental elements, which also adhered to those same guidelines. However, nothing was done to be pretentious or contrived.

We believe the River House is our best example of a signature style that blends the ornament, grace and formality of a historic home into the design of a modern place to live.

Blending Classic and Modern

The trick in building any signature style home is to know when to follow the strict rules of the traditional architectural style that inspired it and when to feel free to deviate from them.

For a fusion of classic and modern that still conveys the impression of a particular classic style, the designer and builder will need to closely follow the prescribed patterns for the desired traditional elements and, wherever a modern detail is preferred, he or she should follow the tenets of modernism: simple, unassuming and minimal.

It is just as difficult to invent a modern detail that will match the historic patterns of a classic style as it would be to find a new serving platter to match an antique collection of dinnerware. A bad choice in either case will stand out and detract from the overall desired effect. For example, many historic classic styles do not have patterns for gangs of large windows because it was not feasible to build a home with a wall of glass at that time. So, when it was decided that the River House would have one wall made entirely of glass, we determined it was best to trim that glass wall using simple modern details rather than impose distorted patterns of a Greek Revival Style. It is better to reproduce classic details where appropriate and to use minimalist details where the classic details will not work.

Just as with Millford Plantation, the exterior and interior details of the River House all come from the neoclassical handbook, except this home was designed with a modern family in mind. From one point of view it is a modern house based on a modern floor plan with airy, loft-like spaces and walls of glass allowing a strong connection to the outdoors. From another point of view, it carries on the traditions of classic architecture by celebrating decorative elements the modernist would scorn. It is then, both classic and modern at the same time.

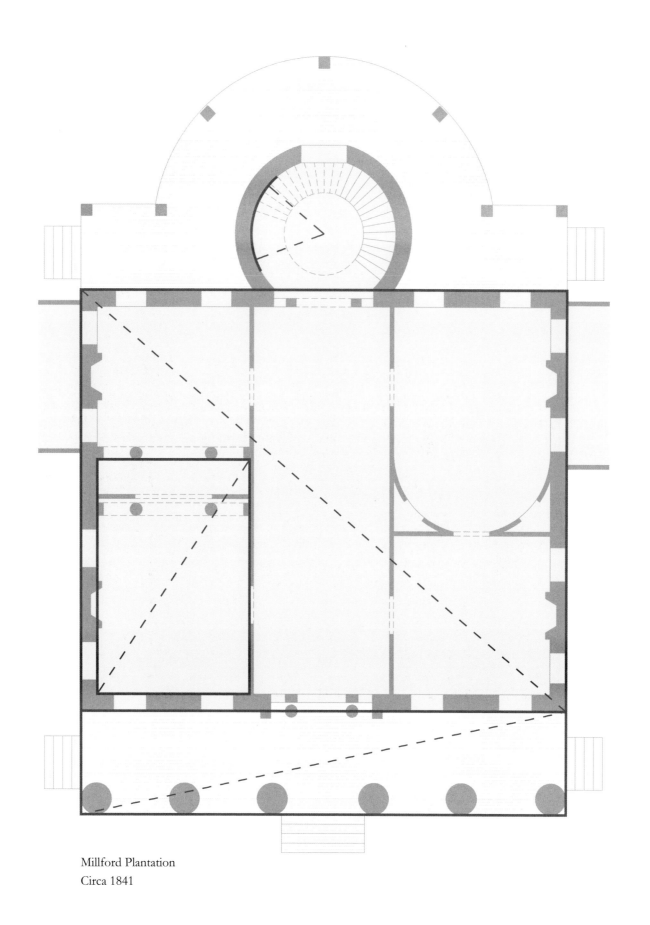

Millford Plantation
Circa 1841

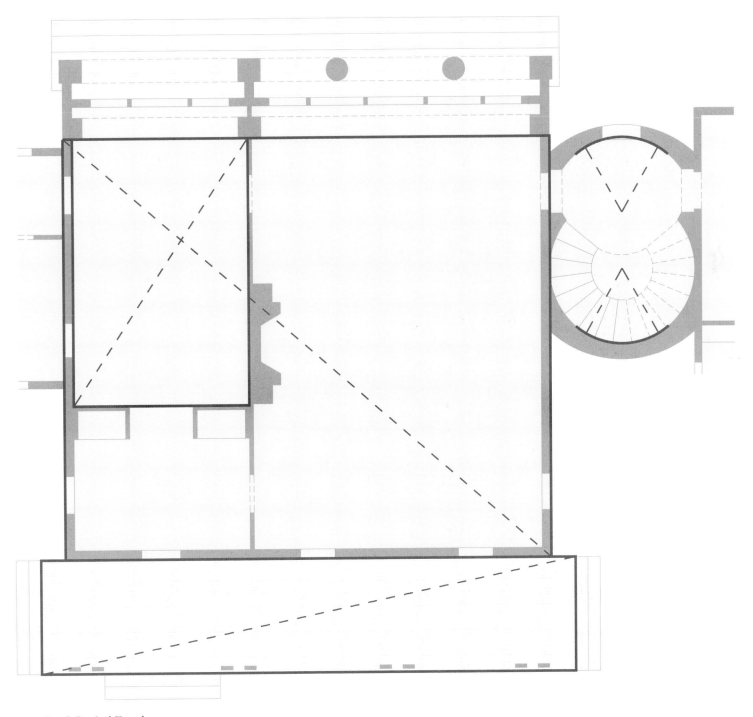

Greek Revival Farmhouse
Circa 2008

REVIVAL

A TWENTY-FIRST-CENTURY
GREEK REVIVAL RIVER HOUSE

*N*othing better exemplifies a signature style that fuses classic with modern than the home we call the River House.

As you can see in the previous floor plans, this modern home is laid out with just two all-purpose spaces as opposed to the symmetrical series of formal rooms found in a classic Greek Revival home. A modernist giant wall of glass rests comfortably behind the classically proportioned colonnade. It faces south and west, filling the interior with the warmth of the sun during those cold and long Midwest winters while also taking in views of the river nearby.

Though the new twenty-first-century structure is ornamented with many exact replicas of architectural details from the historic Greek Revival homes of the South that inspired its creation, this is not a contrived reproduction. It is a thoroughly modern neoclassical house, designed from the ground up to suit the midwestern landscape and the lifestyle of a twenty-first-century household.

STICK

RETRO MODERN & READY FOR A PARTY

*I*nterior *designer Matthew White* has a singular style: a cozy version of opulent—sophisticated yet comfortable and always ready for a party. From Los Angeles and London to this Hudson Valley country estate, Matthew has applied this approach to each of the homes he has created for himself and his spouse, Thomas Schumacher.

Matthew's vision for a guest cottage on his country property led to a cozy cottage not unlike those built after World War II. Often referred to as Stick Style, the architecture of these 1950s cottages was inspired by the Hudson River Bracketed homes created by Alexander Jackson Davis a century before. The economic optimism of the 1950s played an important role in redefining a "country home" as a leisure retreat rather than an agricultural residence. Made with simple sticks of wood and painted with the exuberant colors of the post-war '50s, this style perfectly suited Matthew's aspirations for something simple and playful.

In this updated interpretation, the window trim, porch railing and posts are in the classic stick style but have been lightened up and simplified, and the colors are more pastel than the bright colors used in the original stick style cottages—yet this is still clearly a cheerful retreat.

The open floor plan, with every room flowing into the next or to the outdoors, makes this 800-square-foot cottage feel spacious and meets the requirement of being "ready-for-a-party." A mudroom and a master bedroom, each in its own wing, align with the cross axis of the kitchen/living area, expanding the sense of space. Cathedral ceilings and high windows in every room allow natural light to flow in every direction. While the architectural details are spare, Matthew adds his clever touches of opulence using faux classical ornamentation throughout. The retro kitchen is perhaps my favorite corner of this cottage. Placed at the front of the house, you can almost imagine standing at the sink looking out the window and seeing a 1952 Chevy Bel Air pulling into the driveway. The masterly use of color, attention to detail and customized furnishings all add up to a tiny cottage that lives large.

COTSWOLD

AN ENCHANTING USE OF TIMBER & STONE

*J**ulie and Elliot*** decided that it was time to build a cutting-edge artist studio and guesthouse on the historic Hudson Valley property they had purchased years before. Set high on a hill on their property was an abandoned shack of a house, which they believed was the perfect spot for a creative respite.

Going in, Julie had a strong vision for what the design should be: a romantic, timber and stone structure. As we discussed her vision, the image of an old English Cotswold barn began to emerge. Inspired by the craggy, rural and romantic terrain of Cotswold, England, the original versions of these beefy, rural buildings were made of heavy timber and stone and have survived since the time of Shakespeare.

Timber is an extraordinary natural material with which to build. It is a raw slice of a tree that is merely cut to the right length and width for the structure being built. Because it is not overly machined or manhandled it is said to retain most of the life force of the stand of pine, hemlock, Douglas-fir or spruce timber it was extracted from. Timber is so rich in character that architects consider it a precious material—much like a jeweler would think of titanium.

To continue the metaphor, if timber is titanium, stone is white gold. Stone is an enchanting, picturesque building material. It embodies history because the formation of stone takes millennia; it embodies nature because stone cliffs, stone beds and field stonewalls are heavily populated with every type of wild life; and it embodies craftsmanship because it is a cooperative medium for sculptor and stonemason alike. Stone can be stacked to hold up roofs, carved to create architectural elements and even sliced thinly to decorate floors and wall surfaces.

In my mind, this studio built of timber and stone is a perfect representation of Julie and Elliot's own work and personal style: finely crafted, abounding with life and wildly romantic.

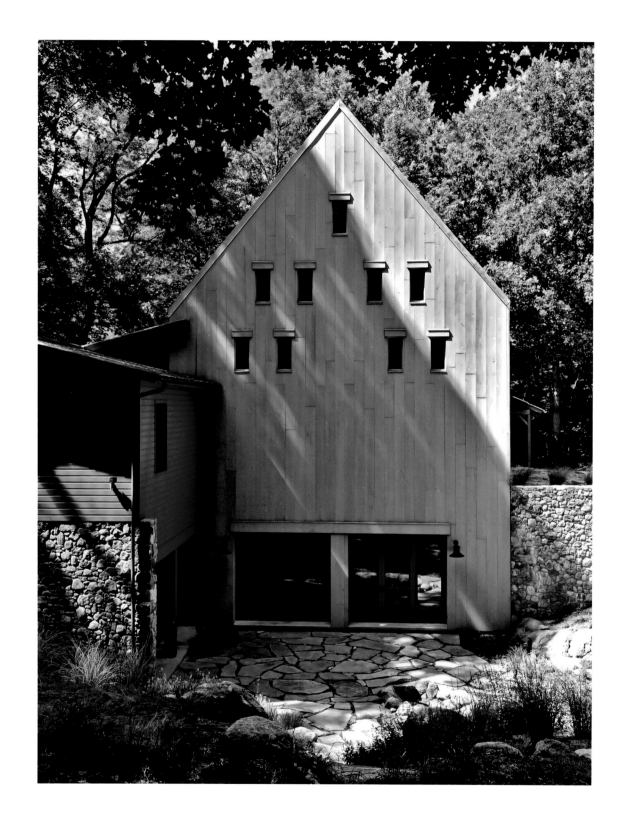

COLONIAL

MODERNIZING A RURAL TRADITION

athy and Michele wanted a traditional classic country home but also a thoroughly modern and Green one. We began with the most classic farmhouse style: the Saltbox Colonial. This style of house has been consistently popular since the seventeenth-century throughout rural America. It gets its name from the shape of the house: an asymmetrical roof resulting in a two-story wall that faces the street and a one-story wall that faces the back. The shape is very reminiscent of the saltboxes used in old Colonial kitchens.

Historical farmhouses are charming to look at but they are notoriously cold and damp in the winter. Today, however, Green designers and builders have a broad range of new building techniques to create traditional-looking homes that will also stay warm and cozy without wasting energy.

This three-bedroom farmhouse consists of two wings that flank a conservatory-like living room. The layout allows the sun to heat up the central living room in the winter and distribute that heat throughout the rest of the house, while the outer wings block the hot sun in warmer summer months. The conservatory uses an oversized version of double-hung windows to create a glassy great room that looks out over the countryside. There is also a deep modern-style overhang that adds to its modern character and also helps to keep the room cool in the summer. Each wing is actually a saltbox of its own, true to the historic proportions and detailing of colonial architecture.

Colonial simplicity is carried throughout the interior with whitewashed walls, simple flat trim, plank flooring as well as traditional architectural elements such as doorways, railings and millwork. It's easy to imagine the house is two centuries old, yet it is also clear that this is a modern and comfortable place to live. Cathy and Michele have created their own signature style—a new classically inspired country home that is energy-efficient and filled with more natural light than any old house ever could have been.

COTTAGE
AN UNPRETENTIOUS HAMPTON HIDEAWAY

*C*ottage Style is an editorial term that is often used in magazines and books to describe designs that use architectural materials and details found on waterside bungalows of New York and New England. There are many romantic paintings of these oceanfront single-story homes fronted by a picket fence, with gardens made up of rose trellises, hydrangea hedges and creeping thyme-covered pathways.

When Fred and Nancy bought their bayside home, Elsewhere, it was an unremarkable and rambling one-story ranch without any of the distinctive oceanfront character of historic East Coast homes. When it was decided the house and garden could use a facelift to better suit their beautiful location, Fred wanted to be sure their property would not lose its quiet, unassuming character. Cottage Style was the perfect solution for just that. No matter how large the home, if you can capture the essence of these humble, stick-frame, handcrafted bungalows with architectural features like cupolas, widow's walks and lanterns, it is both striking and endearing.

Giving Elsewhere a new personality was also a matter of fusing cottage-style architectural elements with a sophisticated modern interior. Interior designer Julia Doyle selected themes that blended cottage-style finishes with unexpected modern designs of tropical woods, high-gloss surfaces and high-tech accessories. Though the property was charming before the renovation (a quiet peninsula surrounded by beach grasses, large specimen trees for shade and deep hedgerows of seasonal and evergreen shrubbery for privacy) there was one final touch that would complete Fred and Nancy's signature style estate. Landscape architect Margie Ruddick was brought in to fuse the classic roses, hydrangea and thyme plantings with a modern landscape of ornamental grasses and wild shrubs. Ruddick's work exemplifies this fusion of classic and modern by expertly blending the tried-and-true with the avant-garde and it works seamlessly with Doyle's design.

Care, craftsmanship and a clear understanding of what makes for a charming seaside cottage is what navigated all the designers on this project. The result is an unassuming oceanfront hideaway–just what Fred and Nancy had hoped for.

SHINGLE

AN "EAST-MEETS-WEST" SHORE RETREAT

Shingle Style is a description of the classic nineteenth- and early-twentieth-century designs that were noted for their sculptural wood shingle roofs and fanciful wood shingle patterns on the walls. This style, favored by architects who designed the vacation homes, oceanfront resorts and casinos of New York and New England, fuses elements from local historic buildings with those of faraway, exotic cultures.

Having spent formative years in the Far East, Peter Wilson wanted to use this shingle-style for his and his life partner's vacation home. Peter's partner, Scott Sanders, is an interior designer and together they decided on a design that would not only remind Peter of his time overseas but would also look "at home" on the eastern shore of Long Island. The home also needed to be roomy and comfortable for entertaining and to accommodate Peter's extended family, who come for long summer stays.

Shingle-style roofs are large and shapely and set the architectural theme of this design. It mimics Thai pavilion architecture with tropical island style roofs that swoop out just before they meet the columns and walls that support them. However, the architectural details on the roof trim, columns and walls are all in the vernacular of its location, resulting in the desired impression of East meets West. The ocean is just a stone's throw away and is best seen from the upper floors, so we carved out the Asian-style shingled roof at its highest point and created an American-style widow's walk.

Inside, the East-meets-West theme continues with more modern interpretations of the shingle-style. Though the tall rectangular windows and doors are classically detailed, their arrangement was inspired by Eastern Shoji screen architecture. By using dark materials, furniture, art and objects imported from the Far East with brightly-colored, mid-century modern American furniture and fashionable finishes, the result is perfectly Ying & Yang—seemingly polar opposite elements coming together and complementing each other through their difference. This is unique to households that pursue and successfully create signature style homes.

NEOCLASSICAL

OLD WORLD ARTISTRY & HOSPITALITY

*A*ll *revival styles* are inspired by legendary cultures, creating strong identifiable characteristics. A Tudor Revival country home, for example, looks ancient with its stylistic nods to medieval England, and a French Empire Revival with filigree details appears quite regal. This classic Revival Style villa adheres to the philosophy of the nineteenth-century originators of this picturesque approach. They believed the style of one's house should reflect the homeowners' aspirations.

Homeowners, interior designer Matthew White and his life partner, Thomas Schumacher, both value old world artistry and hospitality. These are the basis of their signature style. These qualities of life and Italianate architecture are immediately evident when viewing the hillside home they named Otium. Inside and out, it recalls a Tuscan villa where good food and wine are served in perfectly proportioned, artfully decorated rooms and terraces.

This modern interpretation of the Italianate style, however, avoids feeling stiff and pretentious by interjecting a theatrical flair. The front façade is flanked by fanciful turrets at the corners, resembling a proscenium, and the entrance looks like a stage set. The house is laid out like a Tuscan courtyard house. U-shaped arrangements of rooms for living, dining and sleeping surround a double-height indoor/outdoor entertainment space that connects to the surrounding countryside through an impressive wall of glass. The theatrical theme continues throughout the house with White's own designs for wall coverings, light fixtures and furniture, all of which capture the essence of Italianate Revival but in a lighter and more playful rendition.

At the same time, strict classical rules of proportion are adhered to in every room and in each architectural detail to ensure this home will stand the test of time.

By following the principles of classical architecture with an artful eye for décor, Matthew and Tom created a signature style villa—showy enough for friends and family to enjoy while staying true to the style that inspired it.

AFTERWORD

BY DENNIS WEDLICK

*T*he *Classic & Modern: Signature Styles* homes featured here offer an alternative to the one-style-fits-all version of modernism espoused by many in the design field. It demonstrates that twenty-first-century residential design can be far more free-spirited and innovative if designers are open to a fusion of styles. Each of these homes was completed after 2001 and is state-of-the-art construction. Yet, all demonstrate an enduring enthusiasm for history, craftsmanship and allegory.

My first book, *The Good Home*, was published in 2001 and featured the residential designs we produced in the first ten years of my practice. In it, I argued against the sprawl of "cookie-cutter" homes that were of poor quality, lacked integrity and seemed heartless. I also maintained that many highbrow residential designs—either modern or classical—offered little in terms of innovation or real personality. *The Good Home* presented a dozen made-to-order homes commissioned and inspired by creative households who appreciated architecture for its history, craft and expressiveness. However, in order to be affordable, the designs used a limited, off-the-shelf palette of exterior building materials such as asphalt roofs, modular siding, common porch posts and double-hung windows. The minimalist interiors consisted of open floor plans with modestly sized rooms. White sheetrock walls and simple Danish Modern trim were also used as matter of cost-effectiveness.

Classic & Modern: Signature Styles features the residential designs my partner, Alan Barlis, and I completed since *The Good Home*. Like our prior decade of work, this past one brought about another unique collection of homes derived from the aspirations of the owners. However, these clients— many of whom were artists and designers themselves—wanted more than the limited palette of materials and finishes I had developed during my early work. They wanted to explore an adventurous blend of architectural elements to create a "dream home" using a design based on their own stories and predilections—a signature style that was theirs alone.

The homes you see in this book are wonderfully eclectic because we made no attempt to suppress the architectural aspirations of the client, regardless of how unusual or far-fetched they were. What we did do, however, was assure that the designs pursued a genuine use of the architectural elements, materials and finishes that the households were drawn to. Neoclassical details are proportioned like traditional neoclassical details; stonewalls are built like traditional stonewalls; and lacquer paints are applied like traditional lacquer paints.

My favorite part of the work featured here is that so many of our clients really pushed the art of homebuilding beyond "just good building practices". They pursued high-performance buildings—buildings that would last longer, use less energy and be healthier to live in. All use state-of-the-art construction methods; all incorporate Green technologies; and all are designed to be in harmony with their natural environment. Some, like the passive house in upstate New York, were especially innovative. It is credited as being the highest performing passively heated and cooled house in the nation.

The success of the homes presented in *Classic & Modern: Signature Styles* is attributed not only to the creative people who commissioned them but also the talented artists and artisans who worked with us to make our clients' dream homes a reality. Often the work was the result of collaborations with another interior designer or architectural firm such as Thad Hayes Inc., Julia Doyle Design Inc. and the Levy Partnership.

We are grateful to our master carpenters: Tom Letteri, Jim Romanchuk and Bill Stratton. They collaborated from the earliest stages of design to assure the results were attainable.

We also had the benefit of building consultants from every area of expertise. Many thanks go to Donald Kaufmann of Donald Kauffmann Color, Barbara Sellick of Waterworks, Ian Ingersoll of Ian Ingersoll Cabinetmakers and Paul Reidt of Kochman, Reidt & Haigh.

Alan and I hope that through this book you, too, will be inspired to pursue thoughtful, free-spirited and innovative twenty-first-century design that not only reflects your personal sense of style and comfort but also considers the health and general well-being of our planet.